Cashing Out with Confidence

-How To Grow A Retail Food And Beverage
Business -

CHRIS MACKEY

Published 2020

Million Dollar Author

Million Dollar Author publishing
Sydney, Australia

Book Layout © 2020 Business Growth Advisors

Cashing out with confidence -- 1st ed.

Dedicated to everyone who has been told that you are slow at learning.

Written by a young boy who grew up in Griffith NSW, left school at 14 years and 7 months because his Dad said he was really not good at school.

It wasn't until later in life that I discovered that I was not "slow", I was just not diagnosed as dyslexic.

I find it impossible to read the way others do, and spelling is even more of a challenge.

We have other skills which more than compensate for dyslexia.

If you are like me and want to write a book, you will find the way to communicate your authority.

Only when the tide goes out do you discover who's been swimming naked.

— WARREN BUFFET

ABOUT THE AUTHOR

Retail Veteran & ActionCOACH Business Coach

Chris Mackey is a retail veteran with more than forty years experience in senior management roles for a variety of Australia's leading businesses.

His expertise includes National Marketing and Promotion Manager for a top 50 ASX company; General Manager of Campbell's Cash and Carry; launching the IGA Supermarket brand in Australia; and extensive international business operations training.

He now shares his wealth of knowledge to empower others to succeed in running their businesses. As an ActionCOACH business coach, he helps individuals recognize the value of their unique skills and to find creative solutions to their business challenges.

CONTENTS

CHAPTER ONE

REALITY BITES

It was one of those dreary dark Melbourne July days in 2017. I had just set up a workshop which I was running for two retailers. The old saying "If I only knew then what I know now" came to mind. Would I have planned or executed this workshop differently? I guess the answer is no, sometimes you can't plan or try to construct the outcomes, my role is to guide and ask good questions.

Two businessmen had engaged me to help them do some business planning. I didn't know at the time how life changing that workshop would be for all of the participants, including me.

The first step that both businesses had to undertake was loading all the data into the planning software. This process was straightforward enough. Both guys were delighted they had all their information together and the mood in the room was very jovial. We were joking, and just having a bit of fun loading the information into the software. My planning software has the ability to forecast the future based on the information entered into it. The whole process took about an hour and a half at most.

Then the mood in the room changed. After working for another 30 minutes, Frank leant back in his chair, stretched out his arms and said, "Holy hell, if this information is right, I've got a problem in my business in about three years' time! I've just spent a significant amount of money and I really feel like an idiot now."

To put things into context, both of those businesses and businessmen knew their industry. They were not fools, they were smart and successful, but faced with the cold, hard reality of the negative figures showing in the profit and loss from the data entered into the software, Frank was understandably gutted.

Gerald on the other hand was looking at the spreadsheet relating to his business and enjoying a level of comfort in the data he was reviewing. Gerald could see a return on his investment, it was just going to take a little longer than he had expected. The fact that it was there gave Gerald a sense of calmness; you could sense his relief.

I pulled the guys together to talk about what we were looking at. Was the information correct? When anyone is faced with such cold hard realities, especially as in Frank's case, it's natural to question that there may be an error in the data or perhaps the information entered is incorrect or the software isn't calculating properly. These are all natural emotions that people go through when seeing that our livelihoods, everything that we work for, all of our dreams, have a use by date and it's ridiculously sobering.

It was now time to face the reality that data doesn't lie, and the figures were accurate.

Frank and I discussed what it would be like if not for this foresight and what it would feel like to relieve the overwhelming pressure of mounting debt and to stop the downward spiral of his business profitability .The good news was that we were now in a position to do something about it.

For Gerald, we needed to know if there was an opportunity right now to do something. Could he could sell the business as it was before taking on any more debt? These are again significant pressures that business-people are under.

Retailers today, especially food and beverage retailers, do not have a crystal ball to create a vision for the future. So many retailers are still relying on the old methods of retailing which are centred around opening the doors, stocking and presenting your shop well and giving great customer service.

The challenge with this model is that it can be and is, replicated and duplicated by anybody. The Independent sector is also challenged by the marketing budgets of the three big giants; Coles, Woolworths and Aldi that do such a great job.

How can the recipe be tweaked to get a better outcome? What levers can be pulled and pushed? What actions need to be stopped and started so that a different outcome can be manufactured?

Firstly, let's have a look at what products your customers are really shopping with you for and what type of business have you attracted. The answers to these questions will provide the first of the big light bulb moments in fulfilling a reality for you in your business.

Going back to the story of our two retailers, where were they 2 years later and what had changed for them?

Frank had reduced his store's footprint, usually a big no-no in retailing. He had changed his range to give his customers the products they really wanted to buy and not what he thought they wanted to buy.

The "fresh food product" offer was invested into and Frank increased his market share to number one in the community in a category he could truly win with.

Gerald had gone full steam ahead with his investment and his business continues to thrive.

If there was one thing that changed the direction of these retailers, I would sum it up as confidence.

There are external parties that offer leadership on what direction you should point your business but my evidence would suggest that retailers need to look internally for direction. Focus on the customer experience, define your niche and have the confidence to make the changes needed.

You can grow your business, you can check out with confidence, whether that is selling or just reducing your week to four days. The secret sauce is confidence.

Frank and Gerald feel that they are now leading and not following. They love their businesses again and their customers are raving about what their businesses offer.

In this book I will guide you to having the confidence to grow. I will share strategies and processes that you can follow.

Join me and discover how you can cash out with confidence.

CHAPTER TWO

THE OUTCOMES FROM THIS BOOK

There are three pillars to growing your retail food and beverage business.

The foundation of any business is its data. Without data you are flying blind. Data gives you choices and having choices gives you balance in your life. For some, quality data can create a life you love.

Would you board a plane that is flying overseas knowing that the pilots had little or no data? The information fed back to a pilot on airspeed, elevation and the amount of fuel being used is not just important, but your life depends on it. Imagine the stress that a pilot would be under and how quickly they would burn out if they did not have this information?

When it comes to our businesses, we just hope we are okay. We starve our brains of the data that will give us the confidence to make choices.

This book is presented with three key take-aways.

1. Balance - Have the life you love.

2. Freedom - Develop a team that works so you don't have to.

3. Sell for profit - With serenity and forward momentum.

Balance will give you a life you love. Balance creates choices in your business operation. There are some key tools in your shopping cart in creating choices. They are

- a plan to follow so you know how you are performing.
- mastery of your business foundations.
- key financial tools.
- a dashboard that feeds you data and allows for informed choices.

When you don't have choices, you really are at the mercy of your competition and your cash flow.

Freedom from all the jobs in a modern retail business comes from you learning new leadership skills and mastering how to get your team to follow you and eventually act on their own.

There is a famous quote I think of often "Culture trumps strategy every time" and it's true. No fresh ideas or reaction to the marketplace will happen without a culture that supports new thinking.

I'm sure you've heard someone say that their business was not like it was when it started. They can't find or keep good people and if they want something done, they have to do it themselves. Maybe you've said those words.

Later in this book we are going to delve into strategies you can use for your business and why they are critical in getting you to throw out the to do list and help you set up your business to run without you, which is the dream of most people when they go into business at the beginning.

To sell your business for a massive profit is something most owners aspire to. Nothing in retail ever stays the way it was. If you only "follow" on price, then you are only ever second best in the eyes of the marketplace. The reality is many, if not most, independent retailers cannot win on price against the three big chain stores. This is where a lot of readers will put this book down, but I urge you to keep reading. A better path will become clear.

The potential purchaser of your business (unless you are hoping to sell to Coles or Woolworths) will pay a premium for a business that has the ability to adapt to changes in your marketplace.

When you build a business that can adapt to market changes; has a clearly defined niche; is not trying to beat the big three chain stores on price only; is picking trends as or before they happen; and knows what not to do by learning from others' mistakes; then you will have a compelling business for buyers.

Picture yourself with your potential purchaser, a big smile on your face as you say, "Come and let me show you how this business *WORKS*."

Pay day!

Visual
No Choices
Freedom, A team
that "works",so
you don't have to.
Balance,
Have the
life you
love
Data Stability
Confidence
to grow a
Retail
Business
A Living
culture
Adaptability
to your
customers
No Help,
No "WOW"
No
Momentum,
No
Certainty
Sell your business for
a massive profit $

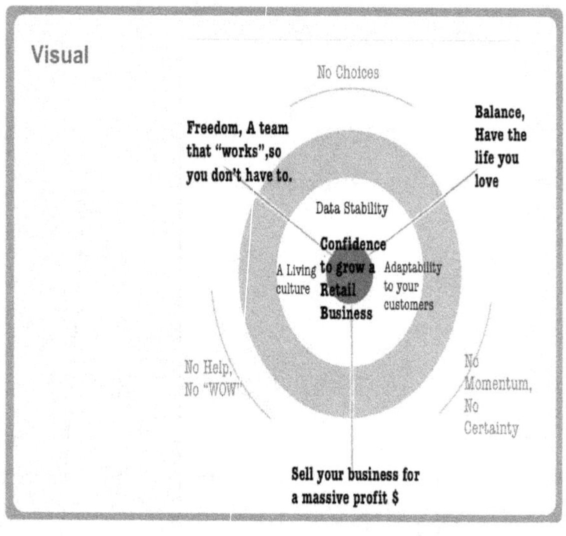

CHAPTER THREE

THE "5 WAYS FORMULA" AS A TOOL IN DATA STABILITY

If there is one universal language that bonds all countries and people together then it is the language of numbers. Wherever you may be reading this book, numbers are the language of a business.

To understand what your business is saying to you, you have to learn to listen to what the numbers are saying.

Usually when I am invited into a retail business, the owner volunteers the information that the problem they have is not having enough customers, to which I ask if they mean there are not enough leads coming in as a result of their marketing activities or because the leads are not being converted into customers? Ten out of ten times, I get the same response; a blank face, followed by "what do you mean?".

Brad Sugars, the famous entrepreneur and founder of the global ActionCOACH franchise, in which I am a franchisee, discovered that customer revenue and profit are outcomes and if we measure the activities that lead to these known areas of business, we can make changes and measure the changes as they happen, on a weekly and monthly basis.

Let's have a closer look at what Brad calls the "5 Ways":

1. *Leads* - How many potential customers do you attract?

    X

2. *Conversion rate %* - How many leads do you convert into customers?

    = **Customers**

    X

3. *The number of Transactions* - How many times a year do your clients buy?

    X

4. *Average $ Sale* - How much do they spend each time they buy?

    = **Revenue**

    X

5. *Margins %* - The Margin your business achieves?

    = **Profit**

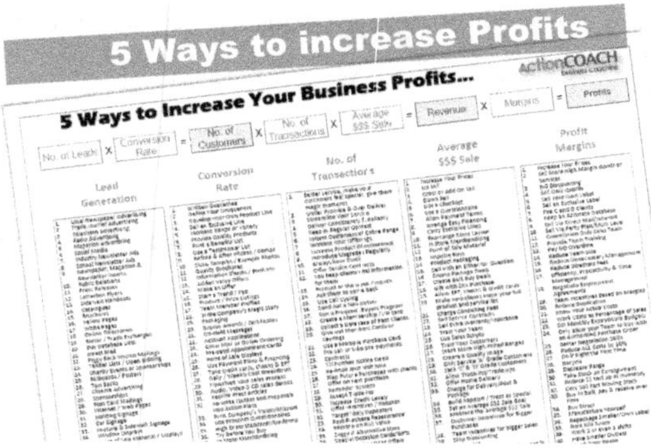

5 Ways to increase Profits

ActionCOACH

5 Ways to Increase Your Business Profits…

No. of Leads × Conversion Rate = No. of Customers × No. of Transactions × Average $$$ Sale = Revenue × Margins = Profits

Lead Generation	Conversion Rate	No. of Transactions	Average $$$ Sale	Profit Margins

Another way to think about the "5 Ways" is to think of compounding bank interest on your savings account. $100.00 initially deposited with an interest rate of 5% will earn you $105.00. When the investment is left in the bank for two years, the 5% interest is calculated on $105.00 and you will earn $110.25. The multiplying effect is what gives business owners who work these numbers the massive success they achieve.

Have you ever thought "why is it that my corporate competition just seems to be so much stronger than my business which is 80% reliant on price to have a great week?"

There are no secrets in retailing, there is only information you don't yet have.

Chain stores know this and work their own version of the "5 Ways". Equally, there are areas where you are performing really well. The point is that if you don't know what your average $ sale is, how do you know if it is growing from the activity you just did or whether it was just from luck?

A retail business I have worked with over the last six months has grown their average $ sale from $35.00 to over $45.00 consistently. To achieve this, we used scripts for the team and trained them on cross and up selling. There was a considerable amount of work done to change the mindset of the staff. You are not being a pushy salesperson, rather, when done with sincerity, you are actually helping someone to buy.

Could you imagine buying some beautiful cheese and getting home to find you forgot the crackers or buying some Gin and not being asked if you needed some tonic water?

If your business is located in a shopping centre, you have considerable passing foot traffic. Your centre management should be able to provide these numbers to you.

You then have a lead number. Although you may not be able to influence this number, you can make significant inroads into your conversion percentage.

As a thought, what does your business look like from a customer's point of view? How open and inviting is it? Have you considered a mystery shopper to give you some real information on what it is like to walk past your store front?

There are endless strategies you can implement. Your competition are testing and measuring constantly.

This is not saying that price is not important because, after all, retail is the most competitive industry there is. If everyone can compete on price, then how else do you grow? Knowing these 5 key numbers is a proven method and just by measuring your business activities your numbers will improve.

CHAPTER FOUR

DATA MASTERY

Have you ever noticed how some retailers are so much more successful than others?

Maybe it's just coincidence that the successful retailers seem to know all their numbers. You can ask them anything and the numbers are clear in their head, they can come up with the answer just like that. The majority of us though just get by with what's being deposited in the bank each week.

The language of a business is its numbers. They tell us everything that's happening within our business.

It's amazing that we have so many different languages in the world, but the language of business is common throughout all people of the world and that's why we can trade globally.

In this chapter, I'm going to focus on what we can do about our numbers in our businesses. Having a good working knowledge of data can be scary. A great number of us run away rather than learn what we need to know about reporting and what the business is saying. I totally get that, it can be scary.

Ultimately, we want to be able to read our data with confidence, which leads to fantastic decision making. Decisions made with confidence get you closer to your goals and move you along a lot quicker than a decision based on gut instinct.

I believe the fears and frustrations that the majority of retail business owners have around numbers are based on what they tell themselves; "I'm no good at financial information" or "I just leave that stuff to the accountants, they tell me what is going on" ; and that, in itself, is very sad. Over time, like with any muscle, the more you use it, the stronger it gets. The more confidence you have around the financial management of your business, the more you will want to know about what is going on. Retail is such a fast-paced business and actions you take today have an effect on tomorrow.

I think that we can do a lot to help people become very comfortable with what their numbers are saying about their businesses.

Business owners ultimately fear what the reporting in their business is saying. This thinking just builds frustration and frustration leads to procrastination and becomes overwhelming.

Now is the perfect time for your business to address the fears and challenges that data mastery presents, fears that could have followed you through your life. Otherwise the problems, just like in the diagram below shows, will just keep repeating themselves.

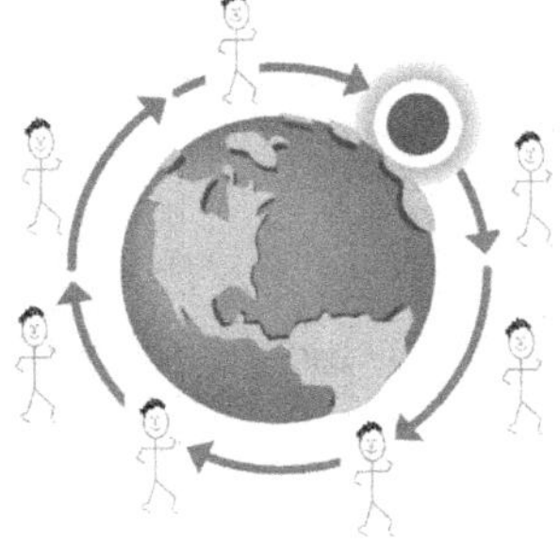

There are three reasons why now is a great time to face your fear of data once and for all:

- Accounting software has never been cheaper and more accessible. Products like Zero are available on a monthly subscription, and even within those accounting software packages, there is entry level right up to ultra-professional so there's little reason for you not to be running accounting software that will give you significant detailed reports.

- Success and growth without data or without the right information is not going to happen. It's critical, if not the gateway. If you want to grow a successful business, you're going to have to have accurate information on your business performance.

- Peace of mind. We've never, in my memory, had so much stress and pressure put on us as business owners. A lot of that has to do with competition and a lot has to do with the fact that business has changed and is ever evolving, and that's a great thing. But imagine the peace of mind you would have if you had better control and a better understanding of the numbers within your business.

While holding a workshop a couple of years ago covering business projections, business planning software packages and budgets as part of business planning processes, I was shocked to learn that the business owners attending had no budgets in place and were not using any budgeting tools in their businesses.

These owners had previously worked for others and had budgets that they were required to meet, and which was a mechanism of reporting to management on how their departments were performing, whether they were meeting targets and if not, what help did they need to achieve their targets.

Interestingly, they used the tools available because their remuneration was linked to the budgets they were given. When I questioned why they weren't implementing these tools in their own businesses now when it was their own and their families' financial security at stake, the response was astounding – nobody had asked them to have a budget!!

Let's take a moment and think about what a budget is and why it's such a valuable tool. The purpose of a budget and the value you get from it, is to tell you what's happening within your business now, historically and what next week and next month should look like.

Think of your budget as a little like driving your car. Should you drive it a bit faster (invest more into marketing or stock), or are you going a bit too fast (need more staff or a bigger selling area)?

It's a complicated topic, but one that shouldn't have you running scared. Consider it a management tool to let you know how you're performing against the goals that you've set. How is your revenue performing? Are you on track to achieve the revenue goal that you set? Are you making the gross profit that you need to cover the expenses that you have, and, ultimately, are you making the profit that you deserve for the investment that you're making?

There are seven disciplines, which I'll detail below, that are invaluable in any modern retail business.

1.   A profit account

Traditionally, a business runs on its revenue versus expenses and what's left is the profit. I suggest that you open a profit account and start saving your profit. Pay yourself first, then pay your expenses. I've recommended this to many of the clients I coach and the difference that it has made is quite significant.

What this forces you to do is to only spend the money you should spend. I haven't come across too many businesses that can be disciplined enough to achieve this but imagine the feeling of paying yourself first. Why wouldn't you? You take all the risk after all and you deserve to be paid accordingly. If there is no money in the trading account after you've taken your profit out, it's going to force you to look at your expenses.

Here's how to do it. Step 1, open a separate bank account. Step 2, budget a percentage for your income; for example, if you've budgeted to make 10% that is 10 cents in every dollar. Step 3, move that 10 cents for every dollar of revenue every week into your profit account.

I promise you that at the end of the year you will have achieved the profit that you wanted because you will have been forced to look at the parts of your expenses you overspend in.

2.   A monthly profit and loss statement.

Set up an accountability session with your accountant, or if you're working with a business coach, make sure that this is the agenda for the first meeting of every month.

A profit and loss statement should be looked at weekly and monthly. After all, it's telling you whether you're making a profit or a loss. The purpose of this report is to give you the motivation to go and do something about your performance.

3. A cash flow report.

The most profitable businesses can fail due to cash flow.

In a retail business you are lucky because you are paid immediately for the goods you sell. Other businesses are selling goods, issuing invoices and then getting paid. Cash flow in our retail business is king.

4. A break-even analysis.

Do you know at what point in any year you've paid for all your expenses? What about a break even for the month? What week of the month do you pay off your expenses and how about each day?

What time in the day do you break even?

If you knew those numbers and say that at three o'clock in the afternoon you had paid for all your expenses, but you were still open until nine o'clock, how would you feel about those additional trading hours?

5.   A debtor and creditor system.

This is normally part of your accounting software package.

As I mentioned previously, the great thing about retail businesses is that you are immediately paid for the goods you sell, but there are still a significant number of creditors. A debtor and creditor system is there to make sure you don't have any surprises and it's important that you look at it. It will enable you to forecast if you will be running out of cash in any week or month. Your accountant will be more than happy to offer you training on the accounting software of Zero and similar packages.

A reluctance to pay for the time is understandable, but in the long run accountants and coaches are there to help you on your journey. What is your peace of mind worth? Make the investment and go armed with questions and you will enjoy and learn from your time together.

6. Profit margins.

It sounds obvious that we should know our profit margins, but do we? Do you know the profit margins of your departments? Do you know the profit margins of the key items within your departments? Fundamentally people sometimes get confused between mark-up and gross profit. If I ask "what is the gross profit of that department and get given a number which I know couldn't be right, I realise the business owner is referring to the mark-up.

To explain, gross profit is the difference between what you sold the goods for, minus what you purchased the goods for at your cost, then divided into the retail price. A mark-up, as the word indicates, is the difference between your cost price, and your retail price.

These two very different numbers are used for different reasons. I personally think that gross profits are more important than mark-ups because you pay your expenses out of gross profit. For example, you have a department with a gross profit of 40% and your expenses for that department are 45%, you can see there is a loss of 5%.

7. Key performance indicators (KPI's)

This is a reporting system that is very important and is missing from so many businesses; I'm referring to a KPI dashboard. A KPI dashboard is made up of five key indicators that the business owner can have at his fingertips that measure performance in the business.

Traditionally, you may have had your weekly sales as a key performance indicator. Instead, I would like you to measure something like the number of leads you generate. Measure something that you can change the outcome of. It's very difficult to change your sales as they are the result of the number of leads and the percentage of those leads you converted into sales. So, by measuring something which is an input, you can really have a lot of confidence in what's happening in your business.

The five key performance indicators can change the way you look at how your business is performing. Can you imagine not having to be so connected to your business but still being in charge and having confidence in what's going on? That's exactly what key performance indicators are designed to do.

You could be on holiday, you could be overseas or studying, and on a weekly basis, your manager sends through what the KPIs are. It tells you that your business generated 5000 leads this week and converted 80% of those to customers. They are your first number and you know that everything is fine. Enough customers were generated this week and your average dollar sale was $35. So now that you know exactly what's going on in your business without just being told what the sales are and what the revenue is, you can do something about it.

I've been in business for over 40 years. Most of that time I spent as a retail executive. Reporting and the use of business intelligence was part and parcel of everything that I did and was a skill that we learned.

If you haven't come into the business world via the corporate route, then I understand the frustrations that you may have, but with a mind that wants to learn and is open to learning new skills, you will surprise yourself how proficient you become at managing your business.

CHAPTER FIVE

THE BUSINESS PLAN

It's amazing how things that you experience in your past magically have an influence on your future. In 2003 I went on an executive leadership program provided by my then employer Metcash Trading. It was an intensive six months live-in course. We were asked to maintain our roles in the company as well as participate in this leadership program.

Little did I know at the time that one of our trainers was going to have such an influence on my life; his name is Major Terry O'Farrell, Australia's Special Forces. It was through meeting him that I found that I truly fell in love with the concept of planning, more specifically business planning. I got an appreciation from spending time with Major O'Farrell of how important planning is. Let's wind back the clock from 2020 to 2003 to the training course that was held in Wisemans Ferry on the outskirts of Sydney, in New South Wales, Australia. Major O'Farrell's role in the course was to help us as business leaders to understand the importance of planning.

Major O'Farrell took us through how the military would execute a plan for something as simple as crossing a bridge. To you and I that sounds quite straightforward but in a military context the planning that goes on behind the scenes to cross that bridge is outstanding. Every conceivable situation is taken into account, not just where the snipers could be hiding to take shots at your troops but also when was the last time that the troops had a drink of water? When was their last meal? Where is their ammunition? What's on the other side? It can be a six-month process that they go through for what seems like the simple process of crossing a bridge.

What really struck home to me though was when Major O'Farrell said "In business, if you put together a plan and something goes wrong, you may lose some money, you may lose some market share, but at the end of the day, nothing terribly dramatic happens. In a military context though, if the planning isn't meticulous, a soldier doesn't come home".

That statement was so profound for me that I reference it regularly in my coaching practice when I'm encouraging my clients to really take the contingencies into account.

That's exactly what the purpose of a business plan is. Another sector we can look at for guidance in this topic is the sports sector. A sports team doesn't take to the field without a game plan.

The greatest teams are those with the best trained players (which is also part of the game plan), a knowledge of how much training to undertake and the knowledge to improve training techniques. Every player knows whose job is it to score the goal, whose job is it to pass the ball or to defend. If it was not for the numbers on the score board, would we know how they were performing? Every sport is meticulously planned, and numbers are used to measure performance. Those of you who are involved in sport at an elite level will relate to this.

If the military goes through so much planning for a simple thing like crossing a bridge and a sporting team meticulously plans everything from the nutrition of its players to the game plan, then I question why in business do we just wing it? We expect to open the doors and wait for the customers to arrive.

We don't like to know how we are performing on our scorecard. Are you moving towards or away from your goals and dreams?

Consider your business as a plane and the cockpit is your business plan. A plane's cockpit is full of levers, gauges and switches and these instruments are all there to give the pilot feedback to keep the plane in the air.

Without this information the plane is likely going to fall out of the air and that is going to cost a lot of lives as in the military scenario discussed earlier. The instruments giving the pilot data on the action needing to be taken is what your business plan does to ensure your business stays on track.

Does every business need to have a business plan? The answer is a resounding yes!

When you're starting out, there is no need for a 50-page manifesto, a simple one-page document is adequate, but you need to know how your business is going. Are you on track to hit your goals from the very first month? If you've been in business for more than three years and you're fairly well established, a business plan is going to give you the tools to forecast and see what the future is going to look like based on your position right now.

If, for example, you have a five year goal to own ten investment properties and you're at year three, and you already have three investment properties, you can be fairly assured that everything you're doing is working, but a business plan will give you a far greater picture of the future. This will help you decide whether driving your marketing a little harder will enable two investment properties to be purchased instead of just one, which puts you on another trajectory for creating more wealth and more generational wealth. That's why I am a fan of a well thought out plan.

A business plan is not about having as much meticulous attention to detail as the military has. It is about applying a lot of the disciplines that the military uses into our business environment.

I emphasise to all my clients and anyone that has graduated in any business, that a business plan is possibly one of the best tools that you can have. It gives you the confidence to know that you're on track. It gives you the confidence to understand what the possibilities are going to look like, what we must take into consideration, structure, strategy, positioning, and to get all these ideas down on paper and into a structure that is useable.

I don't want anyone to read this chapter and be put off or overwhelmed about what a business plan is. It can be as simple as a one-page document, or it could be as elaborate as a 50 page, in depth plan. It's all about what your plan is going to be used for. Are you raising capital for a new venture? Do you need to bring on an investor? Is your business well established and you'd like to consider the future? At what point in time you are going to optimise and sell? Your business plan can be tailored for all these things.

A well thought out plan is going to get you to your goals quicker than any other activity.

46 ·CHRIS MACKEY

CHAPTER SIX

THE CUSTOMER EXPERIENCE

Feeling the awe of going into a store that is doing something new and exciting is inspirational.

Independent food and beverage retailers in this country, and all over the world, have always been the innovators when it comes to customer experience.

Thinking back, most of the modern retail experiences were tested and measured by an independent retailer such as stores within stores, in-store bank branches, and then the chain stores adopted these ideas.

In the late 1980's, Jim Fleming, the owner of Jewel Food Stores, opened a branch in Mt Druitt, NSW that incorporated an attached petrol station. Customers spending a certain amount in-store were entitled to a "cents per litre" discount at the petrol station. This innovation was the first of its kind for a retailer in Australia. Fast forward to today where its unimaginable that the big giants like Coles and Woolworths wouldn't offer a fuel discount with purchases from their stores.

That's just an example of how independent food and beverage retailers have been the incubator of customer experiences.

Unfortunately, a lot of retailers have the mindset that the customer experience is solely based on full shelves in the grocery section that are all faced up like tiny tin soldiers, but it's actually about the human experience. Consumers have an expectation about pricing, appealing store environment and engagement of the senses. Focussing on these aspects is what turns customers into fans.

Have you ever heard of the VAC?

• V stands for our visual senses:
I can see what your store is offering to me clearly and it is communicated well.

A foodie's paradise or the discount king? Consider Aldi Supermarkets; we are in no doubt that they are communicating the Cheapest prices - the store is not fully lit, and stock is often on pallets. Aldi stores at every visual level are communicating "we are cheap, don't expect service".

• A stands for audio:

The environment is welcoming. Music can and does affect our mood. Think about the loud PA addresses at an airport and how that can irritate you more than not having a seat.

• K stands for kinaesthetic:

This means the environment that you've created is tactile. In other words, your customers can touch, smell, and taste. A good example would be when customers can take recipes from a pad placed next to the ingredients used.

We all learn differently, and a lot of businesses fail to appreciate these three ways that we like to receive our information.

When done well, such as when the visuals communicate your intention, the audio within the business is conducive to shopping and the kinaesthetic gets your customers engaged and using their hands, you create an experience that is long lasting and one that your customers will tell their friends, who will tell their friends and on and on it goes.

Have you ever been shopping at fashion retailer Tommy Bahama? It is one of my favourite examples of what to do right and so much can be learnt from this retailer.

All three of the VAC sensors are high in-store and work so well. For example, if you went to buy a shirt, the layout of the store funnels you to move through the whole premises and therefore experience hats, shoes and accessories on your way to shirts.

Once in the shirt section, surrounding the shirts are the belts, shorts, and hats that match perfectly to the shirt you're looking to buy. Tommy Bahama has simplified the process of colour coding and presenting an image to you by engaging all of the VAC principles and building tension for you to swap your cash (or card) for an image and a feeling. Tommy Bahama makes the shopping experience pleasurable and easy by knowing their target market. This is not a cheap retailer by any means. If you've not visited a Tommy Bahama store, I urge you to pay them a visit as the experience is one that is truly inspiring in a subtle, cutting edge, sophisticated way.

If the store experience is done poorly, you will become extinct. Remember the video stores where you could never get a new release? The number of new releases never matched the demand and so they were always out of stock.

The method of having your DVD passed to you from a separate counter next to the exit always felt as if the customer was being treated as a thief. No wonder that when technology such as Netflix arrived and you could stream your own movies, from your lounge, you never visited the video store again.

The hospitality market learnt a long time ago that if you treat your hotel guests like thieves they will live up to your expectation and steal the towels, the bed spread and definitely the little shampoos and conditioners.

The last interaction with your business is what customers will remember much longer than the price. I'm sure you can remember hearing your family and friends tell you about a fantastic customer service experience they had.

Whilst price is important, particularly in a competitive industry like food and beverage, it's not all about price.

Let's fast forward to when it's time to sell your business. If you've created something unique the business is a lot more saleable and a lot more desirable.

We should look outside of the food and beverage industry for what's going on. If a Tommy Bahama business was ever for sale, it would command a premium price compared to your Main Street men's and women's retailer that have been doing business the same way for the last 30 years.

Ultimately retailing will lose to online shopping if we don't work on our customer experience. We have the opportunity to embrace online shopping because many consumers now like shopping this way.

Technology is here to help us. I was reminded of this last week when someone said to me "Well, the ice man doesn't come to your house with a block of ice anymore, you now have a refrigerator". We all have a refrigerator so embrace the technology but also understand that there is a place for the consumer experience. There are customers who don't want to shop online, and our job is to give those customers the best possible experience.

On the 24th of September 2019, the consulting firm KPMG conducted a survey and found that brands that are community led and values driven rate higher on the consumer experience than brands focused solely on building their customer base.

We all know that the Woolworths and Coles loyalty programs are not about loyalty, they're about getting data on your shopping patterns and growing their databases. Retailers that are community based and know what their niche is, are the leading retailers in that niche. Their values are based on sharing information and experiences. These retailers and are thriving.

A European Delicatessen I am working with in my 1-2-1 coaching program (contact me if you would like to learn more) has created a tribe of "foodies". They run regular cooking classes which are sold out in advance. This business shares with its customers how to choose and prepare the right ingredients. Their values are based on community, fun and good food. Does it work? In January 2020 their average dollar sale was over $60.00. A lot of independent supermarkets don't have that result. It can be done and is being done.

I have attached a hyperlink where you can download a copy of the report commissioned by KPMG and if you study it closely, you'll find a lot more information to base any discussion making you consider on facts and not just theories.

Link to KPMG report:

https://home.kpmg/au/en/home/insights/2019/09/customer-experience-excellence-report-2019-australia.html

So, where do we start to improve and grow our customer experience?

As I have previously mentioned, Brad Sugars has said "We've got to start with knowing what the end looks like. It's like the building that you're sitting in today. Someone knew what that building looked like before they built it. So, you've got to think about this customer experience in much the same way."

What is it that you're trying to build? It starts with our dreams.

We never dream enough so I'm encouraging you to dream, be outlandish, live life large.

Dream about the best possible customer experience you could create. Once you have it, we can go about turning those dreams into goals, and goals need to be written down. There's overwhelming evidence that a goal that is written down is 42% more likely to be successful, as **writing it** forces you to get clear on exactly what it is that you want to accomplish. Doing this also plays a part in motivating you to complete the tasks necessary for your venture to succeed rather than it being just a goal that's in your head.

Our simple formula looks like this: Dreams x Goals x Learning.

We know we've got a big, hairy, audacious goal. Now we need to learn things that we don't know. Next time you go to a conference, stay an extra day and get out into other markets. It could be as simple as learning from other industries. Often, we feel that we need to reinvent the wheel, but what we should be doing is recycling other industry ideas into ours.

Start reading books, fill your brain with inspiration and learn how to think differently. A great book that I'd like to recommend is "Think and Grow Rich" by Napoleon Hill. If you haven't read it, I strongly recommend you do before you embark upon growing your retail food and beverage business.

Let's summarise:

Step 1 - Dreams x Goals x Learning. Step 2 - Create a plan.

Dreams turn to goals. Goals x Learning, and after you've learnt, create a plan and then put the plan into action steps.

Often people skip this part and that is generally why plans don't work.

Dreams x Goals x Learning x Plan x Action = SUC-CESS

We have to learn before we earn.

Let's look at the steps for better learning.

Step 1 - Walk in your customers shoes.

When building your customer experience, you have to put yourself in your customers' shoes. When I started my retailing career in the late 70's, one of the first things I was taught was that we did a store walk **every day**. The store walk started outside the shop, either in the mall or in the car park.

Put yourself in your customers' shoes and understand the experience that they're having way before they enter your retail business.

Another really confronting but powerful tool is to engage a mystery shopper.

The last time I did this for a retailer he flatly refused to believe what the mystery shopper said about trying out the store's customer experience. Point blank he said, "That's not my store." I'm sad to say that he is no longer in business.

Step 2 - Training.

You need to be able to replicate yourself, otherwise you'll be tied to the business.

The only way to do this is to invest in your people. Tom O'Toole, the famous baker from Beechworth, Victoria, in response to the question "What happens if I train my staff and they leave?", replied with "What happens if I don't train them and they stay?"!

I think that's a fantastic quote because it helps tell the story around the relevance of training your team. So, think about the customer experience and what type of training your frontline staff need to have.

How will they greet someone who enters your business? How long before the staff greets a customer by their name? How do you train your team on the customer experience?

The answer must lie in the culture that you've created in your business.

Remember that culture eats strategy for breakfast. In other words, nothing will happen long term in your business if the culture is not focusing everyone within the organisation towards a common goal. So, if your culture isn't about the customer experience, then it's going to be very difficult to train your team in the customer experience.

Step 3 - Document everything that you're doing - Everything.

There needs to be a script for how someone is greeted. There needs to be a script that is used when someone is leaving your business.

There should be a standard operating procedure of how stock replenishment is carried out while your business is open for trading. You can document everything, but without a process or a system it is then very difficult to implement a standard.

Do you think McDonald's or Starbucks would be where they are today if it was up to individual team members to come up with their version of how to acknowledge a customer or how to make a coffee Frappuccino? They have invested in processes and systems that deliver a minimum standard of customer experience.

Now I can already hear you saying, "I don't need scripts, surely everybody should know". Unfortunately, they don't. Not everyone has your passion. Not everyone has your life experiences. The purpose of a script is 'when you know something works, keep doing it'.

So, for example, if you greeted somebody as they entered the store with "Good morning", or "Good afternoon", while this is very polite, wouldn't it be better to say, "What brings you out today?"

That question opens up an opportunity for dialogue, which leads to your customer having a two-way conversation with your team, demonstrating that you do care. It's creating that human experience.

The dialogue may continue with "I've come out to get something for dinner tonight."

All of a sudden, you've created the opportunity to engage your customer. You've got the opportunity to help them with a solution and that's ultimately what a business does. It helps people with their problems. So, in just that small example, replacing 'good morning' with 'what brings you out today', which may seem slightly intrusive, opens up a world of opportunity where you can showcase your business.

I remember when Franklin's Big Fresh opened their first store in Leichhardt, Sydney.

If you're not familiar with the Franklin's Big Fresh concept, there was theatre within the store. Animated chickens above the refrigeration were clucking and squawking and bread was being baked and moved around the business on a conveyor belt, all of which not only engaged you visually, it also engaged your sense of smell. Freshly baked bread always reminds me of Franklin's. It should also be noted that Harris Farm Fresh Markets in NSW are now using the bread conveyer belt in their new store layouts, everything old is new again!

I've also had the benefit of going to Stew Leonard's retail stores in America. At the time, Stew Leonard's stores were leading the retail industry for their innovation and in-store theatre.

I've travelled the world and I've gone into retail stores such as Costco and Aldi before they even opened in Australia. I have seen great butcher shops in Sydney, mouth-watering cheese shops in Pyrmont and fantastic fresh fruit and vegetable retailers in South Melbourne. What I have gained is a really good knowledge of what the customer experience is and how we need to work on improving our customer experience or we will lose out to the competitors online.

As you are reading this book, then I know you have a passion as a food and beverage retailer, but I also know that sometimes we need to think about some new ways of doing business. We have to get out of our own way and reinvent ourselves. I want you to guarantee your future, so that when the time comes, you can cash out your business and have a retirement you deserve.

Before that though, I believe you're going to fall in love with your business. After you do the work, your customer experience will be the legacy you leave the industry with.

SEVEN

YOUR CRYSTAL BALL

Your crystal ball; the skill of picking the trend; what's in and what's out.

Some think it's a talent you're born with but it's actually a system and process. In this chapter, I'll show you a more scientific way and how to implement it in your thinking. You will be more informed when it comes to decision making and connecting with your customers to meet their needs and expectations.

Meeting the needs and expectations of your customers, often before they even know they have a problem, is the skill of the marketer and the entrepreneur. We think we know what our customers want but often the facts tell a different story.

To have a retail business that is aligned with your community's needs, you must have new offerings that surprise and delight. Equally, knowing what trend or fad is just about to start or is just about to finish, is the true skill of a modern retailer.

Lots of retailers have the mindset that if you take a risk you may lose money, so they sit and wait for customers to ask for something. This is playing it safe. You're frustrated that your revenue is only slightly up on last year and there's no real growth. That all feeds into your fears of taking risks on new lines and new fads.

In my career in retailing, and when I was a buyer for Coles Supermarkets and for Metcash Trading, the key theme was that new lines or new offers were the lifeblood of retailing. So in 2020 and beyond, don't wait for a company rep to call before you make decisions about carrying a new line. The company rep has gone the way of the dinosaur and there will be fewer and fewer reps calling on your business, especially in regional and remote areas. Even in the metropolitan areas, you're more likely to see a merchandiser than someone who is trained in selling.

The decision now rests significantly with you, the retailer. Remember that you can have anything you want in this life if you help your customers get what they want.

Let's for a moment take what Roz White, Owner of White's IGA Group Sunshine Coast Queensland, is doing in her supermarket businesses in Queensland and add a little bit more science to her process.

Copy this link to your browser to watch the interview:

https://www.youtube.com/watch?v=uPXmX96JTGQ&t=12s

To rate as a retailer, I encourage you to get very familiar with your item movement reports and how to read them. If you don't have them already, create some to know where your stock is at any time and monitor it by setting up some trigger points. You can then be alerted when sales performance of the items that you're taking a calculated risk with start falling below your expectations.

Be aware of other markets and observe the trends and tensions that are being built.

During my career as a buyer for two of the Big Three supermarket chains, a supplier would come to my office to present new lines for consideration to be carried. There were two standout qualities that I was looking for from the presentation. I wanted to be excited by 50% theatre and 50% fact. Much of the decision making of a buyer for a supermarket chain is based on how excited they get about the new product. If I got excited, the likelihood was that my customer base would get excited and therefore purchase, reducing my risk.

You have to give your suppliers a degree of respect that they have spent energy, hours and significant money in investigating and bringing this product to market. They wouldn't be sitting with you if they hadn't already done their homework.

I'd also like you to have a documented process for how your business picks trends and decides on a range of products to have a significant focus on. When you have this information documented in black and white, it becomes a simple process to teach somebody else in your business how to pick trends and new lines that will succeed in your business.

As mentioned previously, when to stop is as important as when to start. Picking trends and finding new lines is exciting and shouldn't be something that you shy away from. As we learned from Roz White's experience in her IGA store, she created a fantastic niche based on local products. Roz could take this one step further by committing to a process and documenting that process. By doing this, if something isn't working out, she would be able to view the flow chart of the process and understand why a product didn't work out and at what point this item or trend failed.

I mentioned before that I have over 20 years' experience as a buyer for two of the major supermarket chains and during that time I also managed teams of buyers in the national corporate office and in all the states. My teams looked after fresh food categories and all the different grocery categories including liquor.

As a buyer, I was impressed a few years ago when I attended an Arnotts biscuit launch of new products for the upcoming winter season. As a company, Arnotts has invested significant amounts of money in repackaging Tim Tams into bite size, bigger size and a range of different flavour combinations. They're doing this to expand their market and to build on the success of the iconic Tim Tam brand, as well as to find new markets to expand into. What struck me so significantly attending this presentation, was the sensory research that happens behind the scenes.

In my ignorance, I believed the new flavours were thought up by people in white lab coats coming up with new ideas and then testing these on the market to see how they perform. I was surprised to learn that a flavour or a new product comes to market when companies like Arnotts utilise sensory listening posts. They notice when a trend is starting. For example, salted caramel flavour, which is so popular right now, is a trend that started in food trucks and the local weekend market stalls. Then it started appearing in bakeries and cafes; this is called a second sensory marker. Until a company gets multiple sensory markers going off consistently, they take no action other than watching - it's like the ripple effect in a pond.

They don't react to the first ripple they see; it sometimes goes all the way to the fifth ripple before Arnotts is confident the trend they are watching is not just a flash in the pan. This trend or flavour profile is actually something that customers are interested in and therefore viable to go into a development phase to bring to mass market.

You can do the same in a retail business. If you are a butcher, look at what is on the reality cooking shows and notice where else you see something similar to the ripples in the pond. If you're a liquor store, what is going on in cocktail bars and what grape varieties are being planted by growers that are experimental?

CHAPTER EIGHT

KNOWING YOUR NICHE

A retailer that has a defined niche just oozes confidence. They know who they really are, and that's evident from the visual communication that customers are receiving about the store and the marketing messages undertaken. A business with a defined niche knows who their business is there to serve. They don't waste money trying to attract people into their business that are not in their target market.

A business with a defined niche is also nimble in their reaction time to customers' needs and expectations. They're ahead of the curve and are flexible. I can promise you that in retailing, nothing ever stays the same. Your ability to change tack, alter, and to find new markets is what is going to allow your business to grow, thrive and prosper with confidence.

If your business's mission is to serve everyone, in other words you're a generalist, then you are serving no one.

When we hear the word niche, we instantly think that means our business can only have one niche. That just isn't true.

A niche is actually about attracting and servicing a piece of the market better than anybody else. Serving the customers that you love working with will result in them loving the whole experience of coming to your shop.

Let's step back and view your business through your customer's lens for a moment. Normally when we are thinking about niche and having a niche of business, our minds run straight away to market retailing. Well, this could be true. Let's have a deeper look at what Aldi has created. Their niche is very clearly defined around cheap. There have been many retailers that have come and gone whose niche was also cheap, such as Franklin's Supermarkets and Jewel Food Stores. Knowing your niche makes your business run very smoothly, from the marketing right through to the cash register.

It's a seamless flow, like a well-oiled machine. What a lot of business owners fear, is that by niching their business, they will lose all other sales. That is a scarcity mindset and there is no evidence that this happens. In fact there is evidence that the opposite happens; that through niching, you can grow your sales because you are known for certain activity, range, and services.

Why bother developing a niche?

There are things that your customers want most from you that you may be completely blind to. Therefore, the process of defining your niche will reveal what your customers really want.

It's also about the survival of the fittest. If you'd like to protect your turf then you need to be the first into that market. If you can see an opportunity then so can somebody else and the first to specialise will succeed.

Speciality food shops such as bakeries and fruit shops are often positioned outside the major supermarket in a shopping mall. The niche of the fruit shop is that they have better quality and range than the supermarket. The reason they are successful is that enough of the supermarket shoppers are looking for that niche which in turn makes the business profitable. The balance of shoppers who buy their fruit inside the major supermarket are doing so just about exclusively on the conviction that both businesses will be price matching each other.

Another reason for developing a niche is when it's time to cash out from your business, a defined niche will ensure that your business works without you, and therefore a more attractive purchase to a buyer.

I worked several years ago with an IGA supermarket in Victoria that wanted to have a vision of where the business would be in the next five years.

The business owner went through a significant and positive mind set change once we started looking into what his niche was. His mind set shifted from a broad range of grocery and perishable items to one more in tune with what his community actually wanted to purchase. He undertook some structural changes and reduced his dry grocery range by 30%.

He then made some visual changes by re-painting and developing a larger footprint for fresh foods. By doing these things he experienced a 10% revenue growth in the first year and a 12% growth in the second year. This year the business is well on track to achieve another 10% revenue growth. There is a significant amount of evidence that niching can deliver a better outcome than being a generalist.

To start the process of understanding what your niche is or could be, you need to determine who you are currently attracting and why. Does your retail business have a broad range of customers, with a dominant demographic you can detect, or is there perhaps a dominant age group? Have you worked out your average dollar spend, and is there a clear trend emerging? At this point in your research it still may not be clear as to who is your niche. A common mistake is believing that we pick the niche we have, when actually 100% of the time your niche picks you. Take heart and don't give up the process of investigating - it is there for you to discover.

The least amount of price competition happens with a well-defined niche because you add so much more value to the experience and that's what customers want. They will pay for a great service and experience. If you remember back to my fruit shop example, consumers who want their fruit and vegetables to last at home for more than two days will pay for this quality.

Once you've narrowed down who you are attracting and why, it's time to think about the market. An example is gluten free products which are a trend right now and a dietary requirement for a lot of people.

The next step is to do a competition analysis. Is anybody doing what you plan to do within your marketplace? If so, do you still want to go down that path? If your answer is yes, you are now building some confidence that your hypothesis is accurate.

Additionally, don't discount having a look in other areas where you are not yet trading. There's nothing wrong with recycling somebody else's great ideas.

Next, identify your ABCD Grade customers; A - your very best customers; B - customers that you are grooming to graduate to your A Group; C – customers that have the potential to be B Grade, but equally can fall to D Grade. (Investment in the C Grade customers should be very limited); D Grade - those customers you should sack straight away as they don't value what you do, they complain all the time and cost you money to serve.

Work out some marketing strategies that talk to your A Grade and B Grade customers about your niche. These are clearly the people that you are meant to serve.

The last and most important aspect of this journey is to understand the investment you will need to make to enter this niche and what will you get for return on your investment.

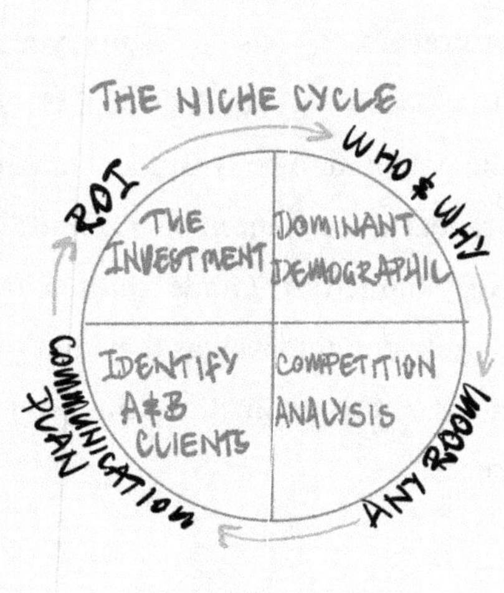

If you're going to develop a niche in cheese for example, then that would require training. Remember this; the quickest way to failure is to think you don't need to learn before you earn. You might also need to buy some new equipment. Do you already have the talent in place, or do you need to recruit new team members?

To summarise, look at who you are attracting and why. Consider the market trend; is someone already doing what you are planning to do in your community or is it really an opportunity for you? Understand how to communicate to your A and B Grade customers about your niche and less to your C and D Grade customers. Look at your return on investment.

As the General Manager of a business called Campbells Cash and Carry, I guided the business to 10% revenue growth and 101% net profit in three years by helping them to define their niche into confectionery and snacks. Through our research and market analysis, we determined that the regular customer of convenience stores wanted snack foods more than they wanted sunscreen and dish detergent. At the time, there were a lot of small wholesalers and we were able to leverage our buying power to do a much better job than the other businesses were doing, resulting in our success.

This is a clear example of how niching into the confectionary and snack food markets made a massive difference to a business in three years.

CHAPTER NINE

CULTURE EATS STRATEGY FOR BREAKFAST

Culture in a sporting team is the difference between winning and losing. A business culture is identical.

History will judge you on the legacy you leave the world, not the car you drive.

What you create is a culture that has lessons, not losses and never stops improving.

Committing to defining your business culture has financial returns as well.

No strategy that you try to implement will ever work without the support of your business culture. Can you imagine starting on a new sales strategy that your team doesn't support? You've lost before you even start. No one should ever have to work in a toxic culture just so they can make ends meet.

I can certainly relate to having worked in a "boy's club culture"; results at all costs. Have you ever heard a fellow businessperson say, "I can't get or keep good people"? In the majority cases the person is in denial about the value of a culture, a defined culture.

Why does your competition never appear to have the same challenges as you? People are attracted to, not repelled by, a healthy culture. To quote Richard Branson, a businessman I admire greatly, "The first thing to look at when searching for a great employee is someone with a personality that fits with your company's culture". Most skills can be learned, but it's difficult to train people on their personality. I think the obvious that Sir Richard is pointing out is his company had a defined culture from the very start, and then he set about looking for great employees. Is this person a good fit for our company culture, because I can teach anyone the technical aspect of this job?

There should also be an expectation that the individual has a level of competency in their skills that matches the position they are applying for. For example, a checkout operator should have a strong grasp of the English language so they can converse with the clients of your business. This employee will not be a good team member if they're not a great fit for the culture.

Where's all this leading and how do you start creating the culture in your business?

What are the first steps? How do you go about documenting what your culture should be?

These are the three steps to take.

1.

Write down the three values that are vital to you as the business owner.

As we go through and create your culture statement, those three values will not be negotiable. We are going to get engagement from your team members but, just to stress the point, those first three values from you are not negotiable, so think hard.

Next, I want you to ask your team to write down on a flip chart, the three values that are core to your customers buying from you again and again. Then ask them for the three values that are important to your team wanting to do their best. Next add the three values that are vital to your business success. That should give you 12 values.

2.

Take those words and look for the commonalities in the replies that your team gave because that's what they feel is the most valuable. Look for those common words and highlight them on your flip charts. Now you need to create statements that support those values.

For example, my business has a defined 14 points of culture and number two is "ownership". I am truly responsible for my actions and outcomes and own everything that takes place in my work and my life. I am accountable for my results and I know that for things to change, first, I must change.

That's just a practical suggestion so that you can create the statements that truly have meaning in your business, to your team and for your success.

There is one golden rule here. If you're going to create a culture, then we must agree not to have any motherhood statements in there. What I mean by motherhood statements is a statement that is full of words that have no real meaning or contribution to your culture statement, nothing of any substance such as "the biggest" or "number one" If the words can't be measured and are just there for filling out the document, then no one will buy into what you have created. It will all be for nothing.

I can promise you if that's the way you do it, this process will not work for you.

3.

The next point I'd like to raise is how you can make this culture statement a living part of your business.

I'm sure you may have noticed, or seen, a culture statement or business promoting itself, that has a defined culture. The creating of the statement is really just the beginning. How to change the culture in your business is the reason you have made this effort.

The secret to making the culture a living part of your company going forward is to allocate one of those culture statements to everyone in your company.

Make them the champion for that part of your culture. What I mean by that is make someone the ownership champion within your company and on a regular basis, for example at a team meeting, that person has to talk to everybody else in the company about how they have lived up to ownership. As part of the team meeting agenda, allocate a few minutes for that individual to talk about what ownership means to them personally.

Another of your cultural points might be abundance. Whoever you've allocated abundance will discuss what abundance to means for them personally in the business. I'd recommend that you rotate what people are responsible for on a quarterly basis to ensure everyone takes ownership over a period of time of all the points in your culture.

As easy as it sounds, it really is important to ask yourself, who do you have to be? What mindset and commitment do you need to have to see this process through?

As Richard Branson pointed out, the culture was a massive part of the forming of his Virgin company. It's the reason people did business with him; his culture was very different to what was normal at that time. Any of you who've experienced a Virgin flight can definitely remember how the staff, the flight attendants, the check-in team, and everything else was a little different. Everyone who worked at Virgin seemed a little happier.

I've worked with a number of businesses now on defining their culture. I recently had some feedback from a real estate business who I was engaged by to help with their internal and external communications. I put the whole team through creating the culture statement as part of a 13-week program. The majority of the employees all commented that creating the culture statement was what they most enjoyed from the course.

It's a very important part of a business and the difference between making it or faking it.

I encourage you to undertake this project as part of growing confidence in your business. It will repay you tenfold for the amount of effort that you put in and will make the difference between you and your competitors.

KEYS TO A WINNING TEAM

Have you ever wondered why some people in your team complete tasks with ease but still seem to be consistently working against you?

You care so much for your people. All that you're after is a fair day's work for a fair day's pay.

We think that everyone has or should have the same values that we do.

The reality is that no one has lived your life other than you. Your experiences and lessons are uniquely yours.

So, what is it that retailers want?

They want to be able to find good people and be able to keep them when they do find them.

It's frustrating to have to do everything yourself in your own business and it's even more frustrating not knowing what you can do to get your team all pulling in the same direction, which is to serve your clients. Without help from your team, there is no "wow" in your business.

There's no way that you can, or should, be present in your business for the number of hours that it's open. Inefficiencies start to cost you money in wages when everyone on your team are is not working together and harmoniously. When you are tied to your business your lifestyle and your family life suffers because when you're not there everything stops or stalls. That reason alone is why we need to learn new skills and the six keys to a winning team.

In Michael Gerber's book, "The E Myth", a must read for anyone in business,

Michael teaches why most small businesses don't work and what you should do about it.

His strong message is working **on** not **in** your business, a key part of which is working on yourself and therefore working on your business.

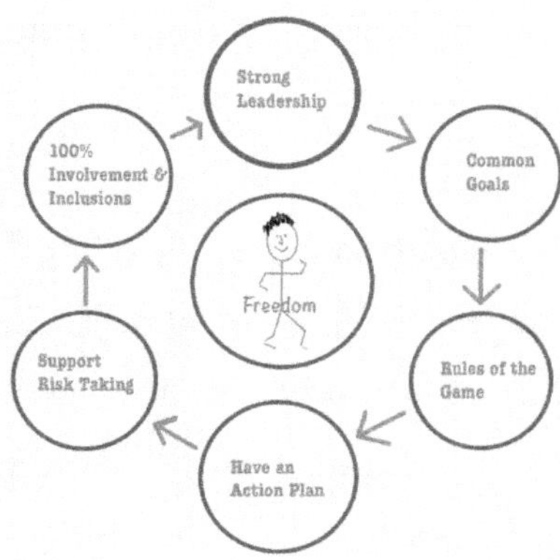

There are six key elements to a winning team:

1.   Strong leadership.

The definition of leadership is the art of moving a group of people to act. Put even more simply, the leader is the inspiration for and direction of the action.

They are the person in the group that possesses the combination of personality and leadership skills to make others want to follow their direction.

Let's take a moment and look at some of the skills a strong leader should have in a retail business.

From my personal experience, one of the key attributes of strong leadership is empathy. The ability to show compassion, the skill to understand at a very personal level what's going on with the person that you're trying to direct.

Another strong value is to never ask somebody to do something that you have not done or could not do yourself.

A simple way to look at that would be to lead by example. If you turn up for work dressed inappropriately, you can expect your team to do the same.

If you're not ready to work at the allocated time of your shift, why should your team, and if you don't speak to your customers and your team politely and respectfully, why would anybody else?

2.   Common Goals.

If you consider the sporting team again, everyone on the team knows what the goal is.

It's usually to get the ball or the player with the ball to the end of the field where he can score the goal. So, in a business context, it's very much the same.

- What are we trying to achieve?
- How are we going to achieve it?
- How do we know when we have achieved it?

3. The Rules of the Game.

Start with the end in mind when considering the rules of the game.

Have a recruitment procedure and system to follow. Building a great team starts with hiring them. Do they fit your culture, your values, your mission and the very fabric of your company?

Defining who your company is, and what the organisation stands for, gives the team the power to perform with the practical tools you have in your rules of the game.

Include detailed job descriptions, example duties, attributes, skills, knowledge, performance standards and some key indicators. These should all form part of your employment agreement.

People want to do a good job; they want to do the best job possible. If we don't set the guidelines and the boundaries for them to work within, it's no wonder we get the results we sometimes do.

So, start with the end in mind when recruiting and the framework for people to work within to achieve the best results.

4. Have an Action Plan.

Start with understanding and auditing your team and ask your team to audit themselves.

You'll naturally find that they often score themselves harder than you would. From that audit you'll come up with an action plan. You'll clearly know where your team thinks that they need to improve, and you balance that with where you think they need improvement. Then create an action plan that's going to help them do their job better.

Employing a mindset that's all about helping your team do the best job they can is a lot more engaging than a business that is penalising in culture.

I'm sure we've all experienced working with someone, or maybe even ourselves, where the mindset is very negative.

Flip that around to a business that creates the coaching style of leadership, and we can then help our team do the best job they can.

5.   Support Risk Taking.

This is key to creating a winning team. Everyone understands the rules of the game, has an action plan, has feedback for areas of improvement and you're mentoring and helping them improve their sales.

Supporting risk taking can be very liberating for the business. This doesn't mean taking ridiculous and uncalculated risks, but if a team member has an idea that they want to try, support that idea. Have the individual work out some pros and cons, ask what is the worst that could happen if the idea fails and then flip that mindset around. Consider what lesson will be learnt.

Small Business in Australia has always been where great ideas are born and that's the reason business owners should have the confidence to support risk taking. Having confidence that the team are all working for the common goal is very liberating for you and it's certainly the catalyst to creating a 'wow' factor within your business.

6. 100% Involvement and Inclusion of Your Team

This is the level where synergy is created! When one plus one does not equal two, but can equal 3, 4, 5, 6 or more. This can take the form of regular team meetings. You have to be disciplined to make sure these meetings take place. These meetings provide an opportunity for everyone to share their wins and focus on the positives, which creates a work place where peoples' input is appreciated and actioned. We have all worked in a business that treats its employees as a necessary requirement but of little value to the business. That type of work place is toxic and theft and sick leave usually run at high levels.

The owners just can't understand that as humans, we all want to belong to something.

The team should share what they're working on currently and what they need help with. Often, when working with a coaching client, I encourage them to have a 90-day action plan, based around the projects that they're working on. I encourage you to do this too. Make sure that this action plan is visible to everybody within the business. That way everyone knows the strategies that you're testing, the ideas that you're implementing, and what the intended outcome of those initiatives is.

This 90-day action plan can also form part of your team meetings, where you share with everybody the progress being made. I'm not advocating that you share information about your profitability but if you are trying a new strategy to increase your average dollar sales, then share it, and make sure everybody knows about it. That's what we mean by 100% inclusion - no surprises.

In my retail background, I worked for a large third generation family owned company called Davids, which had outlets in every Australian state except Western Australia. The business culture of Davids was very insular which meant information was closely guarded within the family and a small circle of long-term employees.

This secrecy extended to the declining health of the business which suffered when the company tried to invest in areas in which it had no expertise.

I also worked for Metcash, the company that eventually acquired the Davids group. Metcash was a business which really did lead by example, from the CEO down. From the time the Metcash group acquired the Davids interests, everyone knew what had to be done. It was known that the business was in trouble and that it was up to the team to turn it around.

It was imperative to engage the suppliers and gain their overall support in order for the business to stay afloat. The strong leadership from the CEO and the board of directors meant that everyone knew the common goals, as dramatic as they were. A lot of the rules were made on the fly, but at least rules existed.

Later in my career at Metcash, I was the key person in launching the IGA supermarket brand in Australia, which was the epitome of a company supporting risk taking. They had a clear vision of what needed to be done and how the independent sector of Australia was being fragmented. Chain stores were continuing to grow because the marketing spend available was being diluted across 27 different banner groups, rather than invested into one banner group and getting every retailer to work together.

That's what I mean about supporting risk taking. There was a high probability that the strategy of launching the IGA group was not going to happen for months and months. It seemed impossible that we could get the retailers to agree to come together as one cohesive group under a banner called IGA, so even knowing the risks, the company went out on a limb to convince our retail customers to come together.

For my part, I had to raise all the funds to launch the group in Victoria and once successful, across Australia. I put together the marketing strategy to ensure that the end consumer also saw the benefit of shopping with this new banner group.

The other way that the business demonstrated 100% inclusion was through our renumeration. The company put everyone from the CEO, right down to the junior team, on a bonus system. The bonus system was all based on the same criteria. Obviously, some earned more than others but the matrix to calculate the bonus was all the same. One of the criteria was that the group had to grow, so not only did you have to grow within the group, but the first criteria was the total company had to grow before you were rewarded.

There were some very difficult times, but it was the first time in my life that I was involved in creating something which became a legacy. On reflection, I really see that without strong leadership, this never would have happened.

I firmly believe the reason that the independent market share in this country is now down to just 7.1% nationally is through the lack of strong leadership that existed in the late 90's. Retailers today, more than ever, need to understand and have the confidence in their own ability and their own strategies, to go forward and not be reliant on leadership from someone like a wholesaler. It's up to you!

FINAL CHAPTER

EXCITING INFO

We are continuing to develop coaching programs to guide retailers in all areas of growing their business.

If you would like guidance, this is where you can get it:

Connect with us on Facebook at

https://www.facebook.com/Mackeybizcoach

Or join our private Facebook group for up to date guidance and tactics on the five ways to grow your business

https://www.facebook.com/groups/Bizgroup5ways

Or follow us on LinkedIn

https://www.linkedin.com/in/action-coachchrismackey/

Or visit our website

https://chrismackey.actioncoach.com/

Or Call Chris Mackey: +61 437474556

www.ingramcontent.com/pod-product-compliance
Lightning Source LLC
Chambersburg PA
CBHW050955050726
47592CB00007B/2574